Copyright © 2023 by Carla Peters
ISBN: 978-0-6457724-0-1

All rights reserved. No part of this book may be reproduced in any manner whatsoever without written permission except in the case of brief quotations embodied in critical articles and reviews.

First Printing, 2023

HOMEWARD BOUND

I am pleased to present my first book, I never intended to write. If I was honest probably like you, I had little self-belief in who I am and what I could accomplish. I looked around and I saw my fellow brothers and sisters fulfilling dreams, being adventurous and living in their truth (or so I believed). At school I was told I would not achieve, I was told I was not suitable, I was told I was not worthy of love and for a long time I held this destructive belief about myself.

Self-confidence is about believing in you and accepting yourself. Each and every one is special and has a purpose and a meaning for being here on earth. For me my environment, my family and my close friends, the natural world became my safe space and during my many adventures and travels I looked to the subtle signs and signals around me. Especially, when I felt broken, lost and lacked trust in my own wisdom. For me, my connection to being in nature and observing, contemplating was vital for my healing process.

So, I dedicate this book to those of us who have been lost, hurt, abandon and rejected. Hold on to hope and believe in your dreams and when the time is right, they will magically unfold for universal timing is everything. Each one of us has a story to tell, be it through words, song, dance, art or touch.

Dedication

To Juniper Rose, thank you, for seeing me and believing in all my possibilities and taking me down the Wayward Path of self-discovery. To BK thank you for your ever ongoing support and loyalty. To my darling husband thank you for being my light when I was lost.

Homeward Bound

Finding the Spirit within

CARLA PETERS

Carla Peters

Yesterday, Today and Tomorrow

Yesterday is but a memory,
Sketched upon my mind.
Today is just one moment in time to dream,
To embrace forever more.
Tomorrow is an opportunity waiting to be fulfilled.
Those dreams we never had the chance to meet.

Carla Peters

Chapter One

The Return

Magic and mystery
Surround me my friends.
No one knows where she hides.
She abides her time.
For the perfect moment.
Setting traps and waiting to catch me unaware.
In my dreams
She appears.
In my thoughts and in visions too
taking me places.
I've yet to explore.

Carla Peters

Life was getting better. The insecurities and self-doubt Lucy endured every day of her life had lessened, and she was slowly coming to know her true worth in this world. It had been some time since she had returned home to her native homeland, let alone the town she grew up in. She wondered how much had changed since her last visit home to bury her mother. It felt decidedly odd knowing her mother would not be there.

Lucy smiled as the memories flooded back. All the hate she had for her mother had diminished during the past years, understanding how hard it is raising children. Not that her mother was perfect, far from it. She recalled the chilly winter nights, eating warm stew and beef dripping on toast to heat her body as her mother refused to turn the heating on to save money. Being the youngest she was always the last in the lukewarm bath water, which by this stage had a film of dirt around the sides of the bath.

Lucy, also a mother to a son with mental health problems, appreciated parenting was not all it was cracked up to be as shown in the glossy magazines and on television. It was demanding work and at times very unsatisfying. Especially when you watched your child miss all the milestones of childhood and teenage years because of social anxiety and depression. Lucy had left her childhood town over twenty-seven years ago and periodically had returned to make the dutiful daughter visits. She wondered how much or if anything had changed since her last visit, surely it had after all this time. She reflected it was a small town, so decided their attitude and ways would not have altered very much or if at all.

It was time for her return journey back home. Lucy boarded the so-called express train to the airport in the early hours of the morning with the other early commuters. The announcement from the speaker advising them they were going directly to the airport but stopped at every station, loudly announcing its arrival and where it was heading next. Having travelled this route so many times, she was not surprised. Lucy stared out of the dirty window and watched the surrounding city become a blur. She looked around at the other commuters and passengers aboard the train. Some were dozing, no doubt catching up on sleep. While others read with their earbuds in their ears. She had packed very frugally, choosing only to take a small cabin size bag with her as she anticipated the arduous journey with its many stops and transit from Gatwick to Essex. Lucy was surprised by how much she could get into her bag and was impressed it did not go over the seven-kilogram baggage allowance.

On reaching the international terminal at Brisbane airport they made their way across the bridge into the departure area and eagerly looked for their airline so they could check in. Brisbane airport always amazed her. How an airport that was considered international could be so small when she compared it to the likes of other major countries she had visited.

Times had changed and Lucy not only had to show and prove she was double vaccinated against the corona, but she also had to carry an international covid certificate. Unfortunately, she had little choice regarding being vaccinated if she wanted to stay employed in her job. Like a robot, Lucy joined the other minions in line and waited her turn.

Gone were the flight attendant welcoming you to the airline, now she was welcomed by a plastic box giving instructions of what to do, she was thankful there was no computer hitch. How she detested this modern world. What had happened to personal interaction. Lucy remembered first time she had flown across to Australia the lady at the travel agency had organised everything. There had been personal interaction, her first flight some time back and how much of an adventure it had been. There had been an element of surprise about what might happen and to whom you would be sitting next too.

Lucy was not surprised in the least when her husband was asked to have his bag searched. It always happened. Lucy was just grateful there was nothing in the bag that should not have been there as she had drummed it into him repeatedly, that he could not bring his Swiss army knife or any sharp objects on board.

As she sat in the airport terminal waiting for the boarding gate to open, she surveyed the people around her and wondered what their stories might be. What adventurous lives did they lead? In the corner were a group of young females overtly trying to impress their male counterparts with gestures of tossing their hair and making the sound of childish giggling to everything the males said. The animated features of the girls reminded Lucy of marionettes; the males seemed uninterested. Lucy wondered where they just friends heading away for a fun time or were they university students looking to uncover the next mysteries of life. She thought about where they were going. Were they going where she was headed? She doubted that anyone ever went where she was going, most people spent their lives trying to escape. Lucy was one of the lucky ones, she had got out as soon as she could of the small, minded town she had grown up in. Not that Lucy disliked it, but sadly it was extremely conservative and traditional, her family had been anything but that.

Her mother was a nonconformist and chose to be different. It was believed through idol gossip the behaviour and actions of Lucy's mother had been passed down and judgement was constantly made about what Lucy was and was not doing and her choices.

Whatever she tried to do, everything seemed to fail. She had felt alone and defeated.

Chapter Two

Brisbane to Singapore

Finally, the call to the board came through. "Will all passages boarding flight ... please make their way to the gate. We are now boarding." Lucy's husband in his usual style jumped up from a dazed state due to being absorbed in his book and erroneously joined the line for first class and business passengers. First class, Lucy thought that would be the day.

On board the plane she was astonished by how small and cramped the plane was considering the price she had paid for the tickets; it had cost an arm and leg. She calculated in her mind the number of shifts and overtime she had to work to pay for the tickets. Had the seats always been this small or was she simply much bigger, she shuddered to think this might be the case. The cabin crew were polite, though not engaging. Her husband was not surprised considering the recent reports in the media about the company. In fact, Lucy's husband had been so concerned he had refused to allow their baggage into the cargo hold as he was certain it would go missing. So yes, they had carefully packed an entire month's wardrobe into a cabin bag with the weight allowance of seven kilograms. As the flight took off Lucy closed her eyes and tried to shut out the world, but the world would not let her. Around her there was constant noise and announcements. Keen passengers excitedly talking about finally traveling after so many years of not being able to due to the corona. Lucy thought what is it with people needing to talk so much, there never seemed to be a moment of silence. If they had something worthwhile maybe but the incessant trivia of ego stroking made Lucy want to scream.

Frustrated she took a deep breath in and with a loud gasp released all the tension in her body and once again closed her eyes and began her meditation. She was not going to allow anyone, or anything, to ruin this holiday for her. Her mind drifted off to faraway places and adventures of ancient tales in enchanted forests with mythical forest animals. The forest and the countryside spoke to her and as often as she was able, she would escape there to recharge her tired mind and body in the coolness of the rainforest close to her home, Lucy found it comforting walking the trails of the ancient land she dwelled on, it freed her soul and mind. Walking and being in nature allowed Lucy to see things more objectively in her life.

Lucy always knew when she was agitated or had received too many stimuli from her environment, electricity charges would pulsate through her body and would spasmodically let out sparks of shooting neural impulses and she became physically drained and unable to concentrate. Her husband always complained that she was irritable all the time. Lucy knew this was true but denied it. Who wants to be seen and thought of as an irritable miserable person. She wondered where her spark had gone. Most days she longed for the days to be over, seeing no value or purpose to her daily existence. But for this brief time Lucy was looking forward to going back to where she had grown up, she was reluctant to call it home. For Lucy home was her security, it was a safe place filled with love and her childhood home had been none of that.

Why was it always duty and responsibility that made you do things she thought, even things you did not want to do. How our minds are conditioned to duty and tasks, order and structure. Where would we be if we did not have routine in our lives? Would we do all the things we dreamed of, or even say the things we genuinely wanted to say as if we had no cares in the world for our actions? Lucy knew she would never say what she thought or felt. She kept it suppressed, festering away like a rotten apple. Lucy was prone to stomach issues and only had become aware of this when her therapist appointed out to her the cause of problems were built up blockages in her sacral chakra.

Why was it that everyone these days thought of themselves as an expert, a self-confessed healer, even a guru of alternative medicine. All you had to do was believe. As much as she tried to believe she constantly doubted their words. Every therapist repeated the exact same phrases word for word as though it came out of a guidebook. Her husband would say if it smelled like a cult, walks like a cult, and acts like one that it does not matter what you call it. If you were forcing people to behave or act in a certain way. Then it was a cult.

Lucy often wondered about this, but she also knew people wanted to be needed and to be useful. The world was full of people in pain, hurting from being lonely, rejected or feeling isolated. There was also a huge depth of trauma in people's lives, she saw this every day at work. People wanted to be seen, to be someone, to be noticed and to have recognition.

No longer could you just be plain old Lucy. Oh no, you had to be goddess Lucinda because Lucy was just too boring. Santa Lucia of Sicily was an early Christian saint who was patron saint of the blind in helping them see clearly. Not only visually but introspectively their thoughts and actions.

Though in Roman folklore Lucy is referred to as the 'light' or 'bringer of light' just as Lucifer is known as the 'light bearer'. Lucifer is also referred to as the 'morning star' and was associated with the planet Venus before his demise and became associated with the planet Saturn, because people linked it to the word satan. The planet Venus like Lucifer is also called Morning Star as it is the first visual planet we see in the morning as the sunrises and the last one we see as the sunset. Therefore, the Lucy's and Lucifers of this world are here to help us see in the dark our true potential and worth.

Not ready to be a goddess how about being a priestess or a queen. As if giving yourself a title allowed you the kudos of being certain of your actions and beliefs. Did they not worry and have doubts like the rest of us? People did not realise to be empowered you had to give up everything including your freedom. Power always came at a price, but most people were unaware at what cost. Lucy knew extremely well. She had been making sacrifices for years. Though nothing outstanding had happened like winning the lotto, then again, she thought that it would be a miracle as she did not gamble. Lucy was predictable, inconsistently predictable is what her husband said she was. Forever changing her mind.

Lucy felt the tug of her husband's hand on her shoulder and glared at him for being pulled out of her experience. She smiled back at her husband not wanting to upset him. She was grateful to him; he had graciously offered to pay for her trip home allowing her peace of mind to relax. Lucy often looked at possibilities and ways to improve her life using natural methods and traditional approaches. Some days she was confused and really did not know what she wanted to be, it all seemed so overwhelming.

Lucy looked at the neatly packed tiny, portioned food in front of her. She had ordered the red chicken Thai curry with rice. She was pleasantly surprised at how reasonable it tasted, but then again it had been several hours since Lucy had eaten. Lucy reflected on her last meal and realised it had been over twenty-four hours since she had eaten. No wonder she was hungry.

Chapter Three

Singapore to Dubai

'Life is a journey of discovery to what we already know.'

Lucy was grateful when the airplane began to make its descent into Changi airport and to have an opportunity to move around. Sitting for seven and half hours in economy class surrounded by endless chatter was not her idea of fun. She was grateful the kids on this leg of the journey had been well behaved, Lucy wondered if this luck would continue. It had been several years since she had been in Singapore. Lucy loved going to the butterfly garden at the airport and watching the koi fish swimming around in the pond. The koi carp are considered connected spiritually to harmony and happiness and in this moment, this was precisely how she felt. As though there was alignment of perfect balance between negativity and positivity in what she was experiencing.

This time Lucy's connecting flight was at a different terminal, she chose to explore the cactus garden. As she swung the door to the garden, she was hit by the intensity of the sweltering evening heat. The garden did nothing for her. However, she did admire the ability of the plants to flourish in such conditions as the arid deserts and the need to rely on so little water to survive. Wandering through the garden she wondered what it was about them she did not like. She realised she was a tactile person, and the cacti were not touch friendly as they were covered with needles. Lucy was surprised when she learned the benefits of cacti included being used in protection spells to ward off intruders and burglars. Though she did wonder if anyone would seriously contemplate climbing up to her apartment to be greeted by a grumpy cat and an overzealous dog, who was more than likely to lick you to death.

The Aztec Goddess Mayahuel was renowned for her connection to the plant agave americana, a cactus plant native to Mexico, the goddess of maguey pulque. An alcoholic drink made from the juices of the agave juices. Her role as patron of a thirteen-day festival of trecena in the Aztec calendar, a time of excess. She was known as the woman with four hundred breasts and her powers were drunkenness, fertility, and revitalisation.

Lucy sat drinking her cool refreshing glass of beer, watching the other travellers passing by and milling around the shops. She wondered which of them were going to be on the same plane as her. Lucy soon realised during the several hours they had been at the airport, she had not heard one announcement being made about flights and boarding. How strange she thought. She quickly glanced at her phone to see what the time was and was surprised by how quickly time had flown by. Lucy made her way to the boarding gate, though her husband was insistent it was not necessary as no call had come through on the speaker. Lucy pointed to a sign showing it was a silent airport and that no announcements would be made publicly.

As Lucy and her husband waited once again in line to have their bags searched and scanned, she wondered who would be sitting next to them. Lucy was pleased her seat had been an aisle seat. The thought of being stuck in the middle seat not being able to get out sent shivers down her spine. Lucy was not used to sitting and being still. Her job involved movement, so to Lucy this was torture or forced rest as her husband put it. She made herself as comfortable as she could for the remainder of her journey and waited for the next leg to begin. Passengers were reminded it was mandatory to keep their face masks on and to politely remind other passengers if they were not wearing theirs to put it on. This was ignored as she looked around, no one was interested in obeying the rule. The journey was unpleasant as it was, without having to endure wearing masks. Lucy had hoped to settle down and have some rest as late evening was now upon her, but the continuous noise of announcements, children screaming and calling out to their mothers for attention made it difficult for her to switch off. Lucy thought alertness can be such a curse at times, but in her work, it was about being alert and aware of any changes, so she found it difficult to switch off, unplug and just enjoy. Lucy found a crossword puzzle and a word search in one of the magazines in the seat pocket in front of her. It had been several years since she had attempted a crossword. She was surprised by how well she did. Finally, after midnight Lucy and her husband reached Dubai.

Lucy was so looking forward to bed. Both she and her husband were exhausted. They had no idea where they were going or where they were staying. In the few days before her trip her work colleague had made her aware as her stopover had been more than eight hours she was entitled to free accommodation and a meal. Lucy had set about making the enquiry but had received no confirmation. On leaving the plane, she was hustled through to the connecting flight area. Ongoing through, she soon realised this was not right and sought help. The staff were helpful and as Lucy and her husband wandered up and down the various levels of the airport in a daze to find the information counter to receive their voucher for the free hotel. After some time and a lot of asking Lucy was grateful to have the voucher finally in her hand. Her husband was amazed at his wife's determination. Lucy wondered why; she knew how to act when required she was a nurse. Most of the time she just wanted a quiet, simple uncomplicated life with no drama, no fuss. For, Lucy work provided more than enough dramas. Lucy and her husband made their way out through passport control and went to find the shuttle bus to take them to the hotel. It was only a short journey from the airport. The concierge eagerly took their bags up to the room. Happy, but tired Lucy fell on to her bed and drifted off.

Chapter Four

Dubai to London

'Adventures are the best way to learn.'
Joel Annesley

Next morning Lucy and her husband returned to the airport for the final leg of their trip. Lucy calculated in her mind the total time it was going to take. She was astonished because it was going to take fifty-one hours, she thought that was more than two days of travelling. She had no other choice; shorter flights were not available in economy class when she booked. Back at the airport they wandered aimlessly through passport and custom control without a hitch. They were super early, so Lucy was not surprised. The Dubai to London flight was so different to the other flights, not in terms of the seating. That was the same, but in the atmosphere and tension around her. The calmness in the previous airplane was gone and was replaced with workers and passengers being irritated and annoyed. Lucy noticed a flight attendant who was a young French girl called Mia. As Lucy observed her working, she soon noticed how the passengers seated behind her were being difficult and rude towards her. Mia remained professional, but Lucy could feel Mia was upset by their remarks. Lucy had hoped to rest on the long flight, but the couple seated in front decided it would be fun to constantly put their seats up and down, which set off the light switch on where her husband was seated. He spent the entire journey with his light flashing the entire trip. She was surprised he had not confronted the couple in front but had gladly chatted to the exchange student who was heading to Dumfries in Scotland after visiting her boyfriend in London.

Lucy finally touched down on home soil. She was pleased to be back. She was also glad her husband had decided to join her. They had made no plans to see anyone or do anything, they had chosen to take each day as it came. This holiday was about revisiting the past, acknowledging, and letting go. It was a time of healing. Lucy had been unable to put her bag near her seat on boarding the plane and now had to fight her way through the crowd to get it down before it disappeared. Lucy thought back to the many times she had been in London peak time traffic on the underground and how she felt like she had been suffocating. It was an experience she was not keen to repeat ever again, drowning in a pool of sweaty human beings.

As they stepped off the airplane, they were welcomed by the stench of stale urine and dirty well-trodden floor. Lucy compared the experience to that of Singapore and Dubai airport which were both clean and fresh, you were welcomed with intoxicating scents to please your mind with pleasant smell of orchid tea filled with Asian spices and fragrances coupled with soft lights, plants and colourful decorated corridors. On arrival staff smiling and nodding happily at your arrival. Here there was a congregation of at least eight security control officers gathered with scowling faces and guns hitched to their belts with a look of boredom as we left the plane.

Lucy and her husband passed through customs without any issues. There was no long queue like they normally encountered at Heathrow. They sat out in the arrival area waiting for Lucy's brother. Lucy's brother had kindly offered to pick them up from the airport. They were incredibly grateful as they did not want to climb on to the train to London, then catching the tube followed by another train to get to Witham. She also had no idea where her brother lived, of course she knew it was in Witham. But what house and street were a mystery to her.

Time ticked by and Lucy began to wonder if her brother had forgotten about her. It had been a while since they had last seen each other. The death of their mother had reunited them, five years previously. Lucy and her husband sat with their two bags waiting on the cold hard dirty plastic chairs and the cold night air blowing through the forever opening and closing doors as passengers left the terminal. Lucy looked around and thought how miserable and unwelcome the whole place was. The people sullen and troubled; she could see no joy on their faces, or peace. She wondered if this sadness was because of the death of Queen Elizabeth the second.

After a twenty-minute wait. Lucy received a phone call from her brother saying he was parked just past the taxi rank. As she stepped out into the cold dark wet night, she saw a car with its lights shining and assumed it was her brother's car. They quickly embraced and jumped into the car as he had stopped illegally on a double yellow line. Lucy sat in the comfort of her brothers soon to be wife's MG and hoped they would be home soon. This was not to be as sometime later her brother confessed, he had taken a wrong turn and they were heading to Leatherhead. Lucy smiled graciously. Finally, they arrived after a two-hour car trip with a detour.

They were welcomed with a huge smile and

embraced by her brother's fiancé Harmonia. This was the first time they had met each other. Lucy liked Harmonia; she had a natural down-to-earth glow about her. This was what her baby brother needed. Someone who was down to earth, practical, and caring. Her brother had always said he would never marry, but Harmonia had won his heart and he knew he could trust her. Lucy was woken in the early hours of the morning by her husband who insisted that it was eight o'clock and was surprised no one was up and having breakfast. Lucy glanced at the time on her phone and saw it was only four o'clock. She turned over and went back to sleep. Lucy finally woke after a restless night, to the sun trying to shine through the grey cloudy sky.

Chapter Five

Maldon

The Wounded Child
I do not understand.
Why me
Why is the sky above so dark?
When I call out
All I hear are cries of sorrow.
from the wounded child.

Carla Peters

Next morning Lucy's brother asked if she would like to go to Maldon. Lucy wondered if she was ready for this. So many memories, so many lifetimes to unfold. Were they all bad, she thought. They had felt bad. Lucy wondered if her role in life was to be a victim or was, she just life's victim. Her friends often told her life was what you chose to make it. But do we get to choose, or does life decide our fate?

Lucy often called upon Hekate for guidance and advice, especially as she got older. What was it with age, which made you question everything. As a younger person she had been so trusting and naïve, how foolish could she have been? Thinking others had her best interest only to use and betray her good nature. Hekate was known for being a Greek goddess in mythology who was associated with witchcraft, magic, and the moon. It is believed she was born around 1600 BCE in Thrace an area covering parts of Bulgaria, Greece and Turkey where she was goddess of the wilderness and childbirth. Later when Hekate became associated as a Greek deity she was aligned to crossroads and the underworld. Hekate was a powerful witch residing over magic, witchcraft, the night, the moon, and necromancy. Having heard the cries of Persephone during her abduction by her uncle Hades, the king of underworld. Hekate went in search for her holding a torch in her hand to guide the way and to lighten the pathway for Persephone. Because of this Hekate, became known as the Goddess of the Crossroads and Keeper of the keys. Pillars called Hecataea stood at crossroads and doorways to keep evil away. These figures were tripartite in shape, with each figure standing back-to-back to be able to look in all directions at potential evil or danger that may have been approaching. For Lucy, these crossroads were associated with decisions and the path we freely chose when our mind, body and emotions are connected to our everyday life.

For nineteen years Lucy had grown up in this small town on the river Blackwater estuary. Having the freedom to wander as she pleased, across the marshes with no purpose or aim in life. If she was no bother and stayed out of trouble, her mother did not care. Lucy had wanted her mother to care for and to be there for her and her sister, but she spent her days in Tom's Cafe drinking endless cups of tea and doing cryptic crosswords from the daily telegraph newspaper, ignoring her children at home. Lucy was never too sure if this was because her mother was trying to impress the other patrons or because she believed she was smart. Lucy struggled with the quick crossword puzzles and seldom did them unless bored. Which for Lucy these days was a rare thing. Lucy's brother dropped her off at the Tesco store and Lucy slowly made her way along the river, or as known locally as the downs. Walking through the quay along the footpath past the old weathered beaten boats and the barges on the decaying ancient moorings and chandlers. As a child Lucy had played here and had imagined the Vikings and Saxons battling on the foreshore with their swords and shields.

She reflected very sadly as she passed the chandler's cottage. How once it had been a nursery school. Lucy had been so happy when her son was accepted into the school. But her son had not embraced this enthusiasm with such delight, preferring to sit in a corner and sulk the entire duration of his day. Lucy sighed and continued. As she walked on, she noticed how everything was different yet still the same.

As she approached the Hythe, she passed the Queens Head and The Jolly Sailor two of the local public houses situated near the River Blackwater where ships, barges and boats were moored. In times past Maldon had been a fishing and transportation town because of its tributaries to the River Brain and the River Chelmer. During the summer months her mother and stepfather had taken them to the Queens Head. While they sat inside Lucy and her sister remained outside in the beer garden overlooking the estuary. They would sit for hours outside on the wooden tables waiting, patiently slowly sipping on their cokes till they had gone warm and flat. Lucy would smash her cheese and onion walkers crisps into tiny crumbs and slowly devour them one by one, trying to make them last. Lucy would watch the other customers come and go as the sunset faded into darkness and the nearby streetlights switched on. The smell of rotten eggs would emerge around them as the evening sun set upon the marshes, almost choking her with its stale stench from the nearby estuary as it worked its way to the back of her throat as the methane gases released themselves as she quietly waited for her mother to finish.

Lucy stopped and admired the sailing barges docked. When she had lived here, they had been private family barges. Now they were commercial and offering tours. Lucy thought about it but continued her walk. As a teenager she had dreamed of boarding one of these boats, just to escape the endless beatings and arguments from her mother and stepfather. Now was not the time or place. As Lucy walked to the end of the pier or commonly known to the local as the extension, was a statue of the famous Byrhtnoth which had been erected in his honour. Lucy remembered briefly studying about him in primary school, but there had been no statue. Bryhtnoth had been the leader of the Anglo-Saxon army in the Battle of Maldon in 991AD against the invading Vikings. An extensive poem The Battle of Maldon believed to have been written at the time or near to the raid depicturing the events of the battle from the Anglo-Saxons viewpoint with accuracy. Bryhtnoth statue looks out to Northey Island where it is believed the Vikings landed.

Lucy and her husband wandered back to the main gates of the prom. It had been built back in 1895 for the people of the town to have somewhere pleasant to walk and relax. The black and white house at the entrance to the prom had originally been a park keeper house. Her childhood friend Freya had lived there, her father was to be the last park keeper to dwell in this house. The house was now a museum, but Lucy recalled many memories within those walls. Freya and her family had lived a simple life, but a happy one. The family had worked as one and they did not live beyond their means. Lucy recalled the warm open log fire constantly blazing even in the middle of summer and everyone huddling around in the chilly winter months. There was always a pot of tea brewing on the stove. She laughed quietly to herself as she remembered how excited they all were when there was digestive instead of plain boring rich tea biscuits in the tin, especially when they had chocolate on them. Lucy remembered how her friend's brother would turn them upside down so no one would know which was a plain digestive or a chocolate one. In the spring months and early summer when the wind was still slightly chilly, they would all pile into the tomato green house and sit in a line on wooden chairs drinking endless cups of tea trying their best to keep warm.

As Lucy strolled up the high street, seeing the same familiar shops. Of, course some shops had changed names and others were abandoned. The facades and look were still the same. Maldon was an old town, dating back to 400BC. Of course, overtime there had been many changes. In 1171 Maldon was granted Royal Charter by King Henry the Second of England. She walked past her old home, well one of them as she had lived in quite a few before leaving for good. This house had been a Victorian house built at the turn of the century as part of housing development in the town for middle class in the victorian and edwardian period. She remembered how the stairs had been very steep and the treads were so narrow that she had to tip toe up the stairs to bed.

The one thing Lucy liked about the house was it was close to the town center and the park. She loved walking and this had been her one enjoyment living in this town. One day she taken their young son Sascha on his tricycle into town to do the shopping. However, Sascha had other ideas and descended down the hill on the way home. Lucy had not been pleased, as her shopping went flying everywhere as she attempted to chase after her son and the tricycle as he rode off resulting in him tumbling down the hill, falling off his tricycle, and hitting his head on a concrete post.

Lucy often wondered if this knock had impacted her son's ability to pay attention in class. As he always seemed distracted and uninterested in life. Her son preferred to spend his days festering in his bedroom only coming out to feed his insatiable habit and to reluctantly eat, whatever food Lucy dished up. Sascha had always been a nightmare when it came to eating. He always refused his food, so many people tried to convince him. But he never paid any attention to them. Finally, at the age of twenty-two he had been admitted into a mental health ward for his eating disorder. The psychiatrist had diagnosed him with avoidant/restrictive food intake disorder or ARFID for short alongside anxiety and depression, plus avoidant personality disorder. Lucy was pleased someone had recognised her son needed help. Though it was a long, slow, and painful journey. Having taken him just over two years being under the mental health act he refused to adhere to the rules and to acknowledge he even had a problem with his eating habits. Sascha had always been stubborn and emotionally reserved. Lucy put this down to him being a Capricorn star sign.

At the top of the town was All Saints Church, where once a month as a young child in the brownies she had held the flag at the monthly church parades. This had been the highlight of her time in the brownies, as most of the time she had been excluded from activities and was constantly given the task of brushing her hair, because it was wild and untamed. How she had hated her hair, it had always been unmanageable. As she looked across the road, she wondered how many people in the town even attended church these days. At some point in Lucy sad life, she had calculated there had been thirteen churches in the town and the exact number of public houses.

In the past, life in the town had been hard and was governed by people attending church to keep their jobs. Lucy and her husband turned and walked into the white horse public house. It had been a while since she had been here. This had been her mother's favourite drinking hole. It was nothing like

Lucy remembered it. Lucy ordered her husband a pint of Guinness, and she had a glass of the house red. It was okay, nothing spectacular. Lucy and her husband sat in silence looking around them. It was cold and empty apart from the middle-aged couple seated in the corner of the bar. The couple with their glazed eyes chuckling away at themselves as they hugged their pints of beer and occasionally glancing towards them.

Lucy in her silence realised how much she had changed. The people here were no longer her people. They looked defeated. They were slowly dying emotionally, as was the town. The town had once been a thriving business with a mixture of wine bars, antique and artisan shops along with the local groceries, bakers, and butchers. This was now replaced with barricaded windows and derelict shops, and what appeared to Lucy to be endless secondhand and reject shops filled with buzzing people. She wondered where hope had gone. Where had the dream gone? Her brother had told her he could not buy in the town we had grown up in and had been forced to move out to Witham. Lucy thought, did these people sell themselves to the devil to be in such a location? As Lucy looked around the town she had once lived in, she spotted a familiar face in the crowd. Lucy was taken back that there was still someone she knew still living here. She knew why, they were a part of an established family tie and had a successful business in the town. Lucy wondered what it would be like to stay in the same town all your life. She had lost count of the number of times she had moved and countries. Though each place had brought new insights and new opportunities to gain experience, plus meet interesting people.

Chapter Six

Family

'Our family tree is like the branches of a tree. We may grow in different directions, yet our roots remain as one.'

That night Lucy and her family went out for dinner at Valenco a local establishment, it had once been a local bank, which was now an eatery. According to her brother the vault remained down in the basement. Lucy was certain that any riches in there would have long been removed. As they ate Stephen recalled how hard it had been growing up and how finding edible food at home had been near impossible. Our mother had not been the greatest mother, or homemaker. Her culinary skills were to be somewhat desired and if she could avoid being in the kitchen she did. Lucy remembered how every Sunday evening her mother had dished up a plain tasteless watery omelette , even to this day Lucy could not eat one without feeling nauseated.

Though times had been hard, Lucy had grown up with her grandmothers around her, unlike her younger brother who had not. It had been just him and mother. Stephen's grandmothers had passed away when he was still young, so he never got to really know them. Lucy had been lucky enough to have been able to divide her time between her two grandparents, each bring different things to their relationship. Her maternal grandmother at some point had found her way back into her mother's life when she was a young girl and had regularly come to stay at the house, often bring gifts. Lucy's adopted grandmother was a homemaker and was about the home, family and building trust and alliances with family and friends.

Lucy's mother had spent much of her time uninterested in parenting, and especially in her son's wellbeing. Their mother worked odd jobs part-time, mainly cleaning. So, she could spend most of her days and nights in the public houses of Maldon. Lucy had gotten out of Maldon as soon as she could. She had felt sorry for her brother.

Her brother had done very well for himself in the past few years since their mother's passing and had entered a relationship with a wonderful young lady who loved and appreciated him. Over time their love had blossomed, and they now lived in a beautiful three-bedroom home in the town of Witham. Lucy and her husband were staying at her brother's place while he and his partner were eloping to Las Vegas to get married. Of course, her brother had welcomed her to join them, but she had declined and said she would meet them and share in the celebrations when they returned home.

Her brother's home overlooked what Lucy perceived as an abandoned pond. Lucy had not seen any wildlife. Not even a sparrow and they were common in the United Kingdom. Stephen's partner had told them to make themselves feel at home. Lucy wondered if she meant this. Lucy looked through the cupboards trying to organise in her mind where things belonged. She noticed a candle sitting on the kitchen table with the words eucaliptus and mint, Lucy smiled at the misspelling from the spanish artisan.

As she continued looking through the cupboards and around the house, Lucy was surprised by the number of different varieties of gin they had. Lucy wondered how many different varieties in the world there actually were. In her research, Lucy found there to be five thousand, four hundred and ninety-eight diverse types in the world. Lucy was flabbergasted. Though Lucy wondered about the accuracy for it seemed to her gin distilleries were popping up everywhere, especially back home in Australia. The United Kingdom alone was said to produce one thousand, seven hundred and twenty-two and was the home of the gin. Lucy was not a gin drinker, in fact Lucy was not a big drinker at all and often struggled to keep up with friends when she chose to go out with them. Lucy did not like to lose control; she also hated the after feeling. She could never have drunk like her mother or taken substances like her son. Oh, yes Lucy was too sensible and practical.

Gin originated to England from Holland and was prescribed for medicinal purposes in 1550 by a Dutch physician. During the 'thirty-year war' soldiers had drunk it to calm their nerves before going into battle. Hence, the name 'Dutch Courage.' On returning home they brought with them this newfound spirit. As its popularity grew people were paid in gin.

Gin is made from berries of the Juniper tree and has a history dating back to over ten thousand years and was even recorded in the bible and used in folk stories throughout the ages as means of obtaining wisdom, protection, faith, and purification.

The juniper tree can live in harsh conditions and can survive on little water. Lucy thought what a versatile plant it must be, so adaptable to so many different conditions. The juniper tree was known to be sacred to the gods and goddess and was aligned to the planets of Saturn and Jupiter and the element of fire. The branches were offered as sacrificial purpose to the gods and were considered sacred to the goddesses. The Greeks would burn the berries at funerals and in homes of those who had died in honour of the Furies, the Roman Goddesses of Vengeance. Alecto, Tisiphone, and Megaera who lived in the underworld torturing sinners. The Roman emperors would have juniper trees planted in orchards and if they withered, they considered it meant an early death or assassination.

Her brother lived on Flemming way. Lucy loved the name as it reminded her of a fleming horse. Their mother had always insisted they were a family who had come from good breeding stock who were into breeding and racing horses. Lucy could never see this as no one around them had even been on a horse, not even at the fairground as their mother had been too tight to spend any money at the local fair when it arrived for the carnival during the week of August. The term Flemming originates from Flanders, an area in Belgium, France, and the Netherlands, from people who were originally of German descent who had travelled across the North Sea to support the invasion of England in 1171 with William the Conqueror. The Flemish people had become an integral part of changing the lives of the inhabitants of England with their skills, contributing more than any other group to the industrial changes of England during the mediaeval period.

Lucy pondered to herself if anyone within the British Isle was pure British sovereignty or had we all become a mixture of neathandedly cultures from faraway places. What heritage ran through her veins. Her mother had claimed when she had been alive, they were from royal stock as in her insatiable effort to find her family genealogy. Her mother had managed to trace part of their lineage back to the Hapsburg family in the black forest of Germany.

Her mother, Mary-Ann, and her brother Marcus had grown up in an orphanage in London at the end of the Second World War. Both children had been left there as young babies and knew little of the outside world before being taken in as foster children to an older couple who could not have children when they were teenagers. Lucy believed her mother had been grateful to her foster parents for rescuing her and her brother, but Lucy knew the damage and trauma had left her mother with mental health issues of trust, abandonment, and hidden abuse from the home. Her mother buried herself in a slow destruction of despair and hatred for the world. Though her mother had not been perfect, not once did she want to abandon her children, she just did not know how to love, for this had never been shown to her.

Chapter Seven

Boudicca

'I am fighting as someone like you who has lost their freedom, I am fighting for my bruised body. The gods will grant us the revenge we deserve.'
Boudicca

Somehow it was decided the next day they would take the train to Colchester. Lucy had wanted to go and see the exhibition at the castle and to wander around the castle park like she had done as a small child during the rare summer months her mother had taken them on an outing.

Having carefully planned the route and the station at which to disembark the train, Lucy was somewhat mystified when her husband had suddenly decided to get of a stop earlier and then on disembarkation had no idea where he was or how to get to the castle or the centre of Colchester. Lucy found this very perplexing and wondered if her husband had other ideas or plans, he had not told her about.

The train journey had been good and had arrived on time at Witham train station with its attractive floral tubs of geraniums in refurbished beer barrels making the visitors and locals feel most welcomed. On board the train, Lucy noticed how clean and spacious the seats were. They even had plugs and universal serial bus sockets to charge your electronic devices as you made your journey across the country. For them it was only a short trip to the town of Colchester. Lucy tried to recall if these functional items were installed in the trains back home in Australia, but she could not remember.

Colchester originally had been the City of Britain in AD49. Though, when the Romans conquered England and took claim to the lands of the trinovantes people it was later moved to London by the Romans. This was because it had a better advantage of being closer to the sea for trade and was a brand-new construction without any past history to tribal clans.

Colchester castle began its life constructed with love and dedication as a temple to Claudius between 49 and 60AD. The temple was seen as a sacred offering and gift to the emperor of Rome. The only people allowed inside were the priests. During this period, it was considered the largest building in Roman Britain.

Following the invasion, the temple became a monument to the emperor of Rome and a place of worship and dedication to him and his successors. Off course over time and endless battles, the castle fell into ruins and was sold off.

After the Boudicca revolt in 60-61AD it was left in ruins for many years before William the Conqueror ordered the construction of the castle during the period of 1069 and 1076AD to be built on top of the temple foundations. However, in 1080AD William ordered the building work to be stopped because of the threat of a viking invasion.

What interested Lucy was Boudicca in her visit to the castle. Queen Boudicca had caused so much destruction and terror during her period of reign destroying major cities and towns such as Colchester, London and St. Albans whilst making the principalities of Rome look weak in their power to claim, control and maintain power over nations and countries such as the British Isles.

So, who was Boudicca and why was she important to the heritage of Britain, even its future? Lucy considered what power Boudicca could have held to have been able to put together such a powerful and resourceful army to have been able to command such respect from her troops and the surrounding communities to lead an uprising that ultimately would change the fate of England. Without doubt Boudicca certainly was an assertive and confident woman who knew her own worth and that of her people. In Lucys mind she certainly was a leader.

Lucy was more than happy to stay out of any debates, discussions or conflict. She hated being seen and being drawn into debates and arguments. Her family and friends would constantly tell her she could not sit on the fence, and choices had to be made. How she detested this. She knew this was the libra in her, the sense of fairness and justice. Always weighing up both counts of an argument or situation and seeing the good in both. Nevertheless, Lucy admired Boudicca and her tenacity, her strength to take on the challenges she faced. She equally respected and supported her friends who voiced their viewpoints. Lucy believed everybody had the right to be heard.

Lucy pondered what it was actually like to have been a queen at this time. What was Boudicca role as queen, what were her responsibilities? What was her purpose to her community? Boudicca had stood up and had become accountable, even when things seemed impossible. Lucy thought for a moment, had it been revenge at what they had done to her and her two daughters or was she making a political statement in trying to preserve her inheritance and legacy she had created with her husband Prasutagus.

After the death of her husband, Boudicca watched as the Romans raided and pillaged her home, her community, their land. Prasutagus had bequeathed half of his wealth to his wife and daughters and the other half to Emperor Nero of Rome in the hope of appeasing him. Alas, this was not to be.

During this period in history the Romans had come to claim and conquer every corner of the British Isles and under Roman law females did not have the right to inherit property or land.

Boudicca was angered, by the way her people were treated and the conditions in which they had to live. For woman and even men without assets you were merely slaves. Boudicca began speaking out against the injustice facing them. Lucy considered was it the public humiliation of being stripped and flogged of her title, her wealth and her respect as a leader of her community or was it knowing her daughters were forcibly raped that caused the Iceni queen to rise like a phoenix from the ashes to find the strength to fight for justice. What was she fighting? power, justice, truth, freedom. In her pursuit for fairness for all, she had become one of the world's first female feminist activist against a patriarchal system of injustice and brutality against women. Unfortunately, abuse and exploitation are still seen today around the world. Woman and the disadvantage are not being heard. Though more women are making a stand and voicing their rights.

Today her statue is seen by millions in London and a recent addition had been placed within Colchester, where many people walk by unaware of her contribution to Britain and to the liberation of womans capability.

Boudicca was and is a symbol of freedom, justice and courage in the face of tyranny after leading her army against the romans in AD60. During this time, she gathered tribal members from the Icenic and Trinovantes to overtake Colchester in her bloodshed.

Lucy wondered if this had ever been Boudicca's intention as the Icenic tribe were fen people from Norfolk and Suffolk region of East Anglia of the British Isles, living a simple modest life as agriculturalist, pottery makers and traders of wool. Their main source of income was from cultivating wheat and barley as their staple supply.

Lucy recalled how her mother had said their family had come from the fens. Was this why she loved wandering the marshes of Essex because it felt like home. In ancient Egypt, Sekhet was the goddess of meadows, marshes, wetlands and the life of fields. But here the Icenic tribe connected and worshipped the lunar goddess Andrasta; she was said to be a powerful and fearful goddess who was both the goddess of fertility and love. She was also the warrior goddess of victory, ravens and battles and like the Celtic goddess Morrigan in her dark phase.

The fens are like that of the Netherlands with its endless hedge less fields stretching four hundred thousand hectares throughout East Anglia region. These boggy fields and marshlands are rich in biodiversity and ecology with their neutral and alkaline water system giving protection and habitation to over thirteen thousand, four hundred and seventy-four species of plants. Included in this are twenty percent of some of the rarest wildlife in Britain and thirteen percent of the rarest species in the world living within these fenlands. Lucy was astonished by such diversity and richness contained within this land. She recalled her school days and began quoting the line from the Tollund man by Seamus Heaney

'In the flat country nearby where they dug him out, his last gruel of winter seeds caked in his stomach. Naked except for the cap, noose and girdle, I will stand a long time. Bridegroom to the goddess, she tightened her torc on him and open her fen. Those dark juices working him to a saint's kept body.'

Lucy had always enjoyed this poem and had found it intriguing and mystifying at the same time. That the rich peat nutrients could preserve a body from so many centuries long ago to tell a tale, to reveal the past. Life and death persevered forever more.

The Romans believed the British celts to be gallic or barbarians' tribesman. They were not, they were just simply homo heidelbergensis people who lived within a small community of hunter gathers who had infiltrated Britain from across the continent of Europe. Most of the skirmishes within these tribes were against neighbouring tribes and clans. The Icenic tribe were of Germanic heritage.

Chapter Eight

Andraste and Victoria

'Don't be intimidated by what you don't know. That can be your greatest strength and ensure that you do things differently from everyone else.'

Sara Blakely

The locals at this time believed Boudicca was a priestess of Andraste, while others believed Boudicca was herself Andraste. According to history she was an Icenic war goddess. The name Andraste means the invincible one or victory. Boudicca before going into battle would invoke the goddess for good luck and safety, she would say a rite in her honour before releasing a sacred hare hoping the opponent would kill the hare. Therefore, giving favour and kindness to Boudicca. The symbol for Andraste was that of the hare and ravens. The hare, despite its rapid movement, is about slowing down and understanding our own intuition, acknowledging the stillness inside of us and trusting in ourselves.

During battle Boudicca would cut off the breasts of her female enemies and stuff them in their mouths and offer them up as a sacrifice to Andraste who was known to accept blood offerings from animals or humans. Like Hekate, Andraste was also a lunar goddess and held the three aspects of womanhood; maiden, mother, and crone. Andraste also had close links to the Irish Goddess Morrigan.

It was rumoured she lived in the grounds of Epping Forest in the ancient woodlands in a sacred grove around Essex and greater London. Lucy wondered why anyone would pray to such a deity, but when she thought about the time and history, she knew life in Britain was cruel and brutal. Andraste was not seen as a cruel goddess, but one of moving forward from diversities in one's life and to the changes we must go through. Chaos and the unknown enable us to be stronger individuals because of our struggles. Lucy knew what it was like to struggle and could relate.

Of course, the Romans had their own goddess of victory, and she was called Victoria. The Roman Goddess Victoria stood for victory and success over death in war. Lucy pondered on how much the Roman empire had conquered and changed so many parts of the world. Yes, there certainly must have been quite a few battles. Victoria during this period was associated with the planets Jupiter as well as Mars and because of this she was therefore worshipped by the Roman army as their protector. The Romans at this time had strong beliefs surrounding the planet Mars, believing it would give them strength and courage under any circumstances to defeat their enemies.

Having studied astrology Lucy was aware of what these two planets represented, and the power contained within them. Statues and temples were scattered throughout Rome in her honour. Jupiter being the planet of luck and growth. Seeing new opportunities. The energy of Jupiter in the solar system is said to be twenty thousand times that of the earth's energy, being the strongest of all the planets. Jupiter brings in the power of good fortune, luck, and healing prosperity. These days Zeus rules over Jupiter instead of Victoria.

Mars energy was about confrontation, aggression, physical strength, and ambition to succeed. In astrology Aries being the first house is seen as displaying leadership and warrior spirit. Being competitive and physically active. No wonder the Romans admired Victoria. As, Mars was the god of war and was also ruled by Aries with the need for survival, animal instinctive and sexual desires. We must remember sexual desire is not always about intimacy or the act of sex, but the energy it creates to release a feeling of connectedness to a source of conscious awareness to bring about feelings of euphoria and pleasure in the act undertaken.

Victoria was one of the last pagan goddesses to succumb to Christianity. Unlike Andraste, Victoria was honoured with wings and feathers or laurel leaves. To the Romans she was goddesses of attainment who could surmount any obstacle or problem. Today at the entrance to Berlin in Germany at the Brandenburg gates stands the statue of the Goddess Victoria on her chariot in remembrance and a symbol of reunification.

Lucy thought it interesting in commissioning of Boudicca statue situated at Westminster Bridge in London to mark the nation's imperial ambitions. It was requested Boudicca face be used to resembled that of young Royal Highness Queen Victoria by her late husband consort Prince Albert.

Beside Queen Boudicca on the sculpture are her daughters bare breasted gripping a spear and the other has her hand outstretched on a chariot with two horse rearing. Adrastea, Victoria and even Boudicca were about fighting injustice and gaining personal empowerment. But ask yourselves whose role it is, who decides that fate. Does that not come with freedom of choice? What is victory? What does it mean today? Is winning, victory or is victory overcoming difficulties and challenges in our lives. Is victory being able to be thoughtful, considerate decent human being with compassion for others and the environment we live in and helping to protect it for future generations. Working with the land and nature and being able to learn from it and its resources. Lucy considered this for the moment and realised nature was and could be just as destructive as humans if challenged or not given the right care. Mother Gaia was known to retaliate with floods, fires, earthquakes, tsunamis, and volcanic eruptions and at the same time she could also be beautiful and creative.

In the book revolt of the angels the author Anatole France speaks of victory being an identity that is evil and has many disguises and is the downfall of the material world. *"We were conquered because we failed to understand that victory is a spirit, and it is in ourselves and in ourselves alone that we must attack and destroy Laldabaoth."* Anatole France – the revolt of the angels (1914) Ch. XXXV.

However, for others victory is an achievement which we attain to meet each day and attempt to master through either dedication, struggle or endeavours to be become a better person or to change our situation or circumstance with respect and harmony.

This is what Lucy had done when she had packed her bags. She alone had made that choice to leave her homeland for a different life. Working along her spiritual path had allowed Lucy to open up, to be challenged. To discover new meaning to life and to appreciate herself and to know her worth and values in a world that was fighting to understand itself amongst the chaos of destruction.

Chapter Nine

Witchcraft

'As above, so below,
As within, so without
As the universe,
So, the soul.'
  -Hermes Trismegistus

As they sat in the castle grounds eating their cheese salad sandwiches and watching a local squirrel running backwards and forwards across the footpath up and down the oak trees while harvesting its food for the coming season. The grassy bank was covered with students taking a break from studying.

Inside the castle Lucy wandered around at the display of old relics gathered over the years from the sites around Colchester town and the witch's exhibition displaying all sorts of paraphilia of how witches were hunted, tormented, and how they had protected themselves. Especially during the Hopkin reign of terror who deliberately and maliciously went about convicting and getting neighbours, friends, kinship, and woman to turn on each other; For what purpose Lucy thought, how quickly we turn on each other to safeguard ourselves, our own principles. But for those who we disagree with or are different to our way of living or thinking we have little time or if any to acknowledge their differences. Why is there such a lack of humanity and victimisation against the female sex in the world. The exhibition focused on witches of Essex, but Lucy knew many other females across England and the British Isle had suffered.

She was silent for a moment and realised they were still being persecuted around the world. Would it ever stop, Lucy thought. As Lucy walked around the castle going from room to room. She took in what the past had meant for these women. Were they witches or just honest women going about their own affairs, who were caught up in gossip and manipulation of their fellow sisters and friends all in the name of profit and power. *'What wicked thoughts our minds and tongues do deceive.'* Lucy felt sick because she had been there, she had experienced blame, accusation and condemnation from friends and peers.

What truly identified a person as a witch? As far as

Lucy was concerned, they were intelligent people who cared for the land and places they dwelled on and did not want to harm anyone, but to work with the law of the lands for protection and preservation. Most were what you call aware or commonly known as intuitive or having psychic powers. Those identifying themselves as witches preferred natural healing and cures as opposed to manufactured synthetic medicines. Not all but many were medical herbalists or healers with a need to help others.

Witches have an understanding beyond time and space, knowing we are beyond the consciousness state of 3D. When we suspend ourselves in the pure physical state, we are operating as individuals and approach life with fear of missing out or not being quite enough and seek to have more. We look at life as good or bad. In the 3D state we have no desire to internalise our world and to understand our reasons or behaviour. Having a deeper understanding of consiousness of 4D required the thinking of greater life exsitence and that our thoughts, opinions and what we said had governance to ideas; be them right or wrong it was a lived experience with compassion. The concept of leading a healthy lifestyle, eating right, understanding our bodies and moon cycles along with the rythmic flow of the seasons and tides of the enviroment. Having purpose, a vision or even a dream to give meaning to life. The exploration of the link between nature, experiences, and emotions and how everything is connected to life, with the ability to understand. True witches saw past themselves and were aware of global consciousness and the need to give back to society.

Lucy thought, how in history it was because you were a female, could swim, or were an old woman deemed you a witch. To Lucy this seemed a lot like sexism and ageism. Other things were talking to yourself or being medically unwell. Lucy thought naivety, greed and superstition had caused the lives of so many women throughout history and fear of being killed. Pointing the finger at someone else was often to save oneself from being accused. Lucy looked at the witches' ball behind the counter and was amazed at how it resembled a modern-day light bulb. Were these women ahead of their time? What, was a witch's ball and why would a witch need one if being so powerful, they could turn someone into a rat or even themselves. Why would they need one? In truth it was a form of protection to ward off evil spirits and ill fortune from the home. As Lucy made her way down into the prison cells, she once again closed her eyes and imagined the endurance these women faced locked up with no sanitation with only the company of vermin. The beatings, the starvations for what. It reminded Lucy of tales she had been told of the communist rule in her husband's homeland of the Czech Republic, fear, and conspiracy. *'Oh, what a tangled web we weave, when first we practice to deceive!!' Sir Walter Scott 1808 (Marmion).*

Matthew Hopkins was an opportunist, under the reign of king James 1 of Scotland and Henry VIII. Hopkins began his self-righteous reign of terror around Essex from 1644 to 1647 during the English Civil War where he tortured endless women and extorted others into giving false evidence for his own profitable gain. King James became obsessed with witchcraft and the devil, believing the land to be possessed. In 1597 he drafted a book called 'Demonolgie'. In his reign of terror and victimisation Hopkins focused on means of deprivation and torture, making women walk for hours on end denying them either rest or sustenance. Starving them until they were exhausted to the point they confessed. Hopkins inflicted pain by cutting them with knives and needles until they bled or flinched. In the center of the castle was a large wooden chair called the 'Clucking stool.' Where the women were thrown into the river or pond. If they floated, they were guilty, but if they sank, they were innocent. This method relied heavily on the woman being rescued. So, what did this self-imposed man consider a person to be a witch. Well, being unmarried, growing herbs, deformity or having a disability and skin blemishes. Lucy considered this and realised today it would mean every woman would have been seen as a witch. Hopkin was what you would call a hustler, falsifying documentation from the government and acting on his own accord for his own profitable gains and pleasure. Hopkin was paid well, during his time between two hundred to three hundred women were estimated to have died all in the name of conspiracy.

One of the first women to be executed was a lady called Agnes Waterhouse from Hatfield Peveril and Elizabeth Lowy's from Great Waltham in England. Agnes was accused by a neighbour and even her own child turned against her. In the end she confessed to having a cat as a familiar. So, what Lucy thought, she had a cat, who she talked to on a regular basis and asked for advice from. In the museum Lucy looked at the replica of Agnes familiar. Was it really a familiar or just a bloody cat? For whatever reason Agnes had claimed it was and that it would turn into a toad named Satan. Her trial took place in Chelmsford, Essex in 1566 she was accused of bringing on illness and killing her husband under the witchcraft act of 1563. Some even said they had heard her speak to the devil. This was not so; Agnes had been speaking in Latin while she prayed. Under the protestant rule of Queen Elizabeth first Latin had been forbidden and everyone was expected to read and speak in English. Now for anyone who is not aware, Hatfield Peverel is a small village in Essex bordering the now city of Chelmsford. Coincidence or not, Waterhouse Lane is the place where the hangman gallows and place of execution were held in Chelmsford.

Lucy considered how often we become susceptible to false or misleading information because of our lack of knowledge or insight. We are so easily led by those in society who have charisma or hold sway over the spoken word as they came across as debonair. She thought for a moment and decided it was during these times we allow supposition to break down our relationships with others and fail to see, hear accurately what is being asked of us. Gossip, misunderstanding and falsehood created can and often leading to politic unrests. The majority of everyday breakdown in society is communication, whether it is what we say, how we say it or just clearly not listening is rooted in the destructive nature of humanity.

Chapter Ten

Candice

"The wound is the place where the light enters you"
– Rumi.

Saturday morning and Lucy had plans to meet her older sister in town for lunch. There had only been twenty months between them. But they acted and behaved so differently, even as children. Her sister Candice had never left the town of Maldon, well except for the few holidays and day trips. Maldon was her home and would always be. For Lucy it had been a welcome relief to escape, she had dreamed of faraway places for a long time. As a teenager she would watch endless episodes of country practice, home and away and neighbours dreaming of a better life in a country far away from her own, where everyone was friendly. Now Lucy lived in Australia, this was her home and she embraced it with welcome arms. Yes, it was different, but she had learned to thrive and grow. Her wounds of the past over the years had dissipated and she had learned to trust her own self and own intuition.

Lucy had agreed to meet her sister at a local baker's called Greggs, which once had been 'Tooks Bakery' in the seventies. Lucy had loved their fresh cream Belgium buns and had always considered this a weekly treat after doing the weekly shopping for her mother growing up. Not that her mother was aware of this. Lucy was disappointed they no longer sold them and was slightly put out as this had been on her return bucket list to the UK. Lucy being Lucy was not happy with going to this local café after reviewing it and changed the rendezvous to a nearby cafe across the road next to the church. Lucy had hoped to spend time alone with her sister, catching up on the past few years. Lucy had not seen her sister since their mother's funeral. However, Candice had decided to bring her partner. Lucy was quite unsure how she felt about this. She had wanted to see her sister alone but was also curious at who this person was that made her sister happy. Lucy was glad to catch up and talk about old times. Their lives had always been so different. Her sister had gone to a special education school and Lucy had gone to the mainstream school. She had not been very academic, but then again had not applied herself either. In her home, learning and education were not of importance. Lucy recalled her mother's words 'if *you were meant to know it you would.*' Lucy had always thought this an absurd response, but then again, her mother had never placed learning or education as a high priority. Lucy remembered her mother refusing to allow her to join the local library. Lucy shook her head. Lucy had done okay in school, but not great either. Lucy reflected how she wished she had paid more attention in class, but she knew it would have made no difference. Her life was destined to be elsewhere. There had been no future in this town for Lucy, she had known this from an early age. Lucy moved to Maldon some time in 1975 when her mother began a relationship with the man who would become her stepfather and change the course of her life and her family's life in Maldon. Lucy moved from her council estate home in Chelmsford to the private dwelling on to an estate known as the poet's estate, where each street was named after famous poets. It was a modest semi-detached home and Lucy hated every minute there, she felt trapped and confined. She felt suffocated. Her freedom she once had was taken away from her. She was no longer able to dance under the stars at night or stand and watch the moon. Each day she was faced with chores. In the evenings she spent countless hours standing holding the old, wired television antenna so her mother could get a signal to watch her programs. Lucy was surprised how her mother knew where all the snooker balls were on the screen, despite having an old black and white television as she refused to pay full price for a coloured television licence.

Lucy felt her life growing up was constantly being challenged, and full of disappointment. All Lucy knew was that every cause or action she had taken led nowhere. Looking back, she realised her actions had led her to exactly where she needed to be and that none of us made wrong choices. It is just a progression of journeys we must make in life to fulfil our predetermined destinies, and this was hers. To accept herself as she was. To honour herself. Lucy wondered why pain and suffering moved us forward and not happiness. Contentment kept us rooted to the same conditions. That night as Lucy slept, her dreams became vivid recalling the beatings from her mother and her sister's rage. The loss of innocence as her stepfather abused her and her sister. Lucy had also wondered what had been worse: the abuse, the victimisation, or the manipulating control of her life from her mother. Growing up without protection, Lucy had to find her own safety. This had meant she went inside herself and buried her emotions, her thoughts and isolated from the world. Lucy had learned very quickly to build an imaginary barrier around herself to protect herself. Lucy did not want to be hurt by society, if her family could harm her what chance would she have in the world? In truth she had felt abandoned by her family and alone. Insecurities, fear, rejection, and loneliness confronted her. Lucy wondered if these feelings were still present even today. The expression 'shadow work' had become a massive thing in the spiritual world and was bantered about as a means of self-healing. Lucy knew every day we were all dealing with our emotions and healing was continuous in this lifetime. For Lucy it was more about acceptance and moving on. She knew she could not change her past, nor did she have to live with it. She was the narrator of her journey.

Lucy looked across at her sister and realised how her sister mirrored her partner, David. It amazed Lucy to watch them interacting together and how they did everything together and conferred on every little detail. As Lucy watched them study the lunch menu, she noticed how good together they were as a couple, this made Lucy happy. Her sister had been single for a long time, giving herself and her own needs over to be there for mother. Mother had always needed and craved attention. Looking back Lucy realised she and her sister had missed their childhoods and the childhood needs of growth and development because of their mother's psychological problems, as well as her drinking habits later in life.

After catching up with her sister, Lucy had planned to take a riverboat cruise down the river Chelmer, but it was late in the season and the river service was not running. Instead, Lucy decided to take a walk around the seawall of Heybridge Basin along the blackwater estuary looking towards Maldon, Osea Island and

Northey Island where the battle of Maldon took place. Lucy and her husband walked along the canal towards the lock and crossed over to the other side. The river Chelmer and Blackwater canal at this site had been constructed in 1796 running through unspoiled rural farmland in parts of Essex for about twenty-two kilometers. In the past the river was used to transport goods such as iron ore, coal, and timber to Chelmsford. For a long time, it had been left, but now it was a thriving tourist attraction with river boats and small sailing vessels utilising the canal between Maldon and Chelmsford in the summer months.

As a teenager Lucy regularly cycled there to escape from life, and the demands of home. Out here she could be free as she walked and walked along the weathered path of fellow travellers over time who had made journeys to Chelmsford, Beenleigh, Mill Beach and Goldhanger using the sea path. The hours spent walking and breathing in the fresh air and picking wild blackberries during the summer months as she passed along the bramble bushes. This gave Lucy such pleasure and delight, filling her stomach and satisfying her appetite. Lucy always felt restricted by her mother, especially in her teenage years. As Lucy had grown in the years her mother became more, controlling, not allowing Lucy to leave her side unless necessary. Her mother demanded more responsibility from Lucy. Lucy now became the parent, she would spend her days cooking, cleaning, shopping, and looking after her much younger brother. While her mother spent her days outside of the home. She did not mind the chores, but there were days when she wanted to be free, she wanted to be like her friends and have fun.

Chapter Eleven

The Mighty Oak

Quiet time, quiet moments
Reflecting off the past
No thoughts, no anguish.
Memories rambling through the mind.
Sitting on the fence between worlds.
What choices do we make.
No rights, no wrongs.
Only moments of passing actions
Caught in life's mysteries.
Silent reflection to where we are headed.
To meet ourselves.

Carla Peters

Early Sunday morning the sun shone through the window hitting her face. Lucy's husband had requested a proper Sunday roast since coming back to England. As promised Lucy had driven them to the cricketer's pub at Goldhanger. Where many years prior to leaving they would spend hours playing dominoes and walking the seawall at Goldhanger. Her husband had belonged to a domino's club and regularly played with a group of other men around Essex. The game of dominoes originates from China and was originally made from the ankle bones of animals, hence why the tiles are known as bones. Of course, today they are made from other sources of material. It was not until the seventeenth century would they make their way to Italy before being introduced into England by French prisoners during the eighteenth century.

As they tucked into the roast, they marvelled at how much they had missed a good old English roast. Back home they just were not the same. Lucy looked at her plate piled high with vegetables, cauliflower cheese, carrots, beans, swede plus roast potatoes and Yorkshire pudding and tucked in, enjoying every bite. The good old British roast was introduced around the fifteenth century under the reign of King Henry VII in 1485 originally for his royal guards who were called Yeomen Warders of the Tower. Where they received chunks of beef as part payment for their duties in protecting the Tower of London. The Tower of London was originally part of the castle where the king and queen lived before it became a high-class prison for aristocracies who had committed felons against the monarchy or country. After attending church on Sunday, which was mandatory, the guards received a roast beef dinner. Following these weekly meals of roast beef, they became known as beefeaters. Traditionally people abstained from eating meats and certain foods on certain days under the Roman catholic and Anglican rulings. However, once a week, being a Sunday, they were allowed to combine and eat meat and dairy together hence it became a celebration and enjoyment to eat a roast with family or friends.

After dinner Lucy and her husband put on their coats and walked through the churchyard to access the Seawall. As they trampled around the fields, Lucy reflected on how surprised her friends had been when she had told them people could wander through farmland where it was classed as a public pathway or bridleway. This began a long time ago and was a perfectly normal method for people travelling on foot to get to the next town or village safely. Lucy embraced everything around her and even breathed in the freezing wind as it hit her chest.

Lucy touched the oak tree and watched as the acorn seed pod fell to the ground. The acorn is said to represent strength, longevity, endurance, fertility, justice, and wisdom. The oak is associated with both gods and goddesses in mythology. From the tiny oak a mighty oak tree is born teaching us about the unlimited potential we have inside of us to achieve and accomplish. The oak throughout history has represented sacredness from its symbolism in the Celtic tree of life to the majestic heights of which it could grow. The ancient world thought these branches reached up into the heavens where the gods resided, and the roots went deep into the earth to the underworld.

Today there are over six hundred species of oaks in the world. Lucy was surprised to find out that these trees were between thirty-two to thirty-five million years old and had the ability to live for one thousand years. No wonder the druids and gods revered this tree. What power and knowledge must be held within the trunk, branches, leaves, and potential in the tiny acorn nut.

Zeus was connected to the oak because during the ancient Greece. During this period, they associated the oak's ability to attract the destructive lightning strikes with being able to remain strong and even withstand the strikes of lightning and thunder. Zeus was the god of thunder. Zeus' sacred oak was the evergreen holm oak and the olive tree.

It is suggested Odin hung himself from an oak tree, but this is debatable as it is also implied the Yggdrasil was an ash tree. What we do know is that the Vikings built their ships from oak and travelled to every corner of the world, making their presence known and for them it was a sign of survival. These trees allowed them to take voyagers to unknown worlds and enabled them to conquer other parts of Europe.

Thor was associated with the Donar's oak which was a sacred tree of the Germanic pagans in what today is known as Hesse in Germany. This was a meeting place for gatherings, rituals, and assembling of chiefs and families from different regional tribes. However, as Christianity grew throughout Europe paganism was frowned upon and was replaced with a new belief system to fit in with the empires being established throughout Europe and the British Isles. The grand Donar tree was cut down by Saint Boniface a English Benedictine monk who was a leading figure in parts of Germany during the Frankish Empire during the eighth century to Christianism the lands. Later becoming archbishop of Mainz and the wood used to make a chapel dedicated to the apostle Saint Peter.

Perun was the thunder god of the ancient Slavs and like Thor, Jupiter and Zeus wielded a thunderbolt of lightning also believed the oak tree to be the symbol of the soul and represented life itself. The Slavic people believed the tree to be a temple and was a holy place in the forest. Disputes and tribal gatherings between people were settled and discussed at the oak tree preventing the spilling of blood or fighting, To the Slavic the tree was about happiness. Lucy's husband was of Slavic origin, and he claimed them to be peaceful loving people.

Cerridwen was a Celtic goddess of the underworld and the moon representing rebirth, transformation and inspiration and the keeper of the cauldron of knowledge where she imparted wisdom, knowledge, and intuition. Her connection to the oak is its roots going deep into the underworld.

Hekate was linked to the oak where she was said to have been crowned with oak leaves and the coils of wild serpents. Hekate was also associated with Zeus, where she was able to keep her powers under Zeus reign because of her loyalty to him during the Titanomachy battle, otherwise known as the Battle of the Gods.

Athena was the daughter of Zeus. She was linked with protection, courage, and leadership. Her symbols included owls, olives, and oak. It is suggested placing an oak leaf in your shoe, so Athena's leadership and bravery walks with you, helping you to face what is ahead of you.

Diana was the goddess of the hunt, wild animals, and woodlands, so it is no surprise she was connected to the oak.

The oak was also sacred to the goddess Brigid and her father Dagda who had close links to the druids. Dagda was part of the Celtic Irish mythology and was a member of the Tuatha De Danann clan as was Brigid who was rumoured to be daughter to Morrigan. Dagda It is believed carried a harp made from oak with the harp having the ability to arrange the seasons in order and command the emotions and wills of men. This allowed Dagda to be seen as a god of order and ensuring everything was in its place.

Even today the oak is symbolic around the world on family crests, logos, and foundations such as the national trust of the UK. We should also remember the proverb 'mighty oaks *from little acorns grow.'* Implying a tiny thought, a seed can create change and lead to something big and what was once insignificant can have the potential to make changes in our lives and those of others. Whatever our view is about the mighty oak, one thing that can be agreed is that throughout history it was revered as the 'Tree of Life' in many cultures and nations around the world. Providing people with hope, faith, and security in their lives.

Lucy continued walking through the barren fields, the crops had already been harvested and the land laid bare waiting patiently for the autumn to end and the winter frost to fall upon the ground. As they made their way to the seawall, they passed by local ramblers making their way back to the village. The cool wind hit Lucy's chest once again; she could feel it was going to be a chilly winter coming. Days prior the news reporter had repeatedly kept saying it was going to be a harder winter than usual and many people were going to suffer, because of the recent price hike in the cost of fuel due to the economic crisis around the world. Another depression was forecast. But for now, Lucy could not think of what was ahead. Secretly Lucy hoped that the financial troubles in England since breaking away from Brexit and current world economics would not impact her life. Lucy loved her life and being here made her appreciate what she had. She had worked hard to achieve her home and to build her career.

*The strongest oak of the forest,
is not the one who is protected from the storm.
and hidden from the sun.
It's the one that stands in the open where it is
compelled to struggle for its existence against the
winds and rains and the scorching sun.*

Napoleon Hill

Chapter Twelve

Mother

"It's not so much what you say that counts, it's how you make people feel."

As Lucy drove across the English countryside in her brother's car to the town of Burnham on Crouch situated on the east coast of Essex. She pondered on what had made her brother scatter their mothers' ashes in such an out of the way place. Lucy could not ever recall her mother ever going there. At best the public transport from Maldon had been infrequent.

She recalled the days prior to her mother's passing. They had been holidaying in Europe on Lake Como in Italy enjoying the late Italian summer sun when Lucy had received the phone call to say her mother's health had deteriorated and she was in hospital. Had Lucy cut her holiday short for her mother, no. Lucy knew leaving her holiday early would not have achieved anything and what could she do. Her mother had been slowly dying for years and the treatment had long ago ceased to work. The cancer had spread throughout her body, and it was now up to nature and her mother's own willpower whether she chose to live or die.

Lucy had arrived a few days later into a cold, grey, wet, and miserable England to visit her mother in hospital. Lucy saw her mother in the cold stark hospital room void of any warmth or attempt to make it inviting for someone who was nearing the end of life. The friendless hospital room reminded Lucy more of a prison cell with its pale green painted chipped walls with no windows to look out. Not that there would have been much to see, but sunlight would have been welcomed. After all her mother was dying, clearly management did not consider it necessary for those who were dying.

Lucy recalled doing her nurse training at this hospital and as she looked around at the baron coldness of the hospital room. To Lucy it felt like death was upon them. She was relieved to be where she was working. From what Lucy could gather the health service in the United Kingdom was struggling and had been so for many years, with less and less funding from the government and no pay rises for the past several years. It had taken its toll on nursing staff who had walked out of the profession. When Lucy had done her training years back, she was lucky enough to have a subsidiary bursary payment from the government to complete her qualification in nursing. This allowed her after three years to leave university with a qualification that was recognised worldwide and to be debt free. Training had been replaced from hospital based to university degree. Nurses now focused on critical thinking, rather than knowledge gained from direct training in the hospital setting. Lucy had been able to achieve hospital practical skills coupled with university knowledge and critical awareness.

She had watched her mother struggling to walk and had requested the assistance of the nurse. Eating had become a challenge and made her feel nauseated, her words were soft and quietly spoken. Right in front of her Lucy could see her mother was fading away. She was no longer the dominating, controlling, harsh woman she once had been. As she had sat in the room with her sister and brother. It had been the first time in several years that we as a family had been all together, her mother had made a passing comment on this. As Lucy surveyed the room, she could see on her mother's face the determination to keep going even if it were just for one more day. Lucy's mother had always been a fighter and never gave in. It was something she admired about her mother. Lucy just could not be bothered. Lucy was gifted, or least she felt she was where patience, persistent and resilience were called for. Her mother had taught her these skills, by denying her so much as she was growing up. Lucy could also be very stubborn and at times had rejected opportunities. Lucy contemplated how hard it was to love and hate someone at the same time. Lucy loved how her mother had made herself sufficient but hated the fact she resisted at all costs asking for help. Lucy thought her mother saw this as weakness or resistance in asking for support and guidance. Lucy concluded it was a lifetime of rejections and endless disappointments. Lucy's mother was a woman who would not conform to societal rules and regulations and in her youth was quite a free-spirited girl forever getting into trouble, living of free love, drugs, and rock n roll and in her mother's case country western music of John Denver, Jonny Cash that Lucy had to endure as a young child. Her children had been less adventurous in this area. Lucy wondered if it had been the endless beatings or the fact they just were not interested. For the past few years, her mother had lived for travelling around the Essex countryside escorting the hospital transport driver in collecting other cancer patients to their appointment for the oncology department. Lucy's mother did not drive and was more than happy to be the back seat driver directing what and where they should be going and which route. Her favourite pastime was reprimanding drivers about their ability to drive. So, in the years of her endless trips to the hospital for chemotherapy and doctors' appointments, this became her mother's happy place of supporting the other cancer patients and giving them confidence and hope to continue even if it was for one more day. Each session her bag was filled with goodies for herself and the other patients to enjoy. Mum's death had changed us all. The news of their mothers' death came as no great surprise. Years of endless self-inflicted abuse of inadequate eating and excessive drinking had taken its toll on her mother's body. Her body had been slowly deteriorating for many years and during this time her mother had gone through major surgery after being found with a ruptured bowel due to bowel obstruction. They also discovered she had liver damage from drinking and smoking. Lucy was not in the least surprised. After being told there was nothing more they could do, her mother had made the trip out to Australia to see Lucy.

Her brother had been left homeless and feeling abandoned at an early age when the property had to be returned to the housing association as their mother had removed his name from the people who lived there. The following months had become a blur for her brother as he was executive of her state, he set about orgainising her funeral and sorting out their mother's home and finding a place to call home. Their mother had been a hoarder of what both Lucy and her brother considered junk. Piled high around the tiny bungalow were endless china ornaments, old records and recipe cuttings out of old magazines.

In the coming years, her brother moved on and had managed to turn his life around with the help of his friends and had secured a new life with new work prospects and a wonderful partner to share his life with. Lucy could not have been prouder of him. Her sister had become independent and was making her own decisions around her life. Lucy also noticed she was less angry and more reactive to life.

Chapter Thirteen

Oysters & Pearls

When you turn your attention to the limitless, the irritation seems small compared to the sun and moon and stars. When you imagine the infinite, you're touched by your infinite self.

Annie Kagan

Next to the town of Burnham runs the river Crouch for twenty-eight kilometres to the mouth of the North Sea winding its way through the wilderness of the Essex countryside. Where like the rest of the Essex coastline Burnham is covered in wetlands, mudflats and salt marshes giving it opportune for various bird life such as the brent geese, oystercatchers, egrets and redshanks and other local species to breed.

As Lucy walked the seawall, she looked into the grey

murky water with the glistening sun hitting the water and making it sparkle, she wondered if the sea was still full of mullet, sea bass, sole, herring and other aquatic life as in days gone by. The town of Burnham was well known for its oysters and creating a source of income and livelihood from oyster farming for the locals and neighbouring villages. During the reign of Charles 1st, oysters were a decree under the royal charter who gave exclusive rights to the Mildmay family in 1661 to harvest. Since then, the rights to the oyster beds have been leased to local companies.

Lucy had never been much of a seafood eater, but she did know they were a useful source of magnesium, zinc, copper, and vitamin D. They were also high in antioxidants and therefore were particularly good for preserving mental health, brain function, reducing stress in the body and supporting healthy aging. Though important for our health it was crucial not to eat too many as the consequences could be unpleasant as her husband had found out. When he came down with the vibrio infection after eating a bad oyster, that put him off eating them for many years.

Oysters are living sea animals and can live up to twenty years. Scientists have been able to obtain deoxyribonucleic from pearls and trace them back to the original source. Oysters eat accumulation of algae, phytoplankton and other small food particles from the oceans and seaways and by doing so help keep the oceans and waterways clean. Therefore, they are environmentally useful to the diversity of the ecological system. However, over the past two hundred years there has been a considerable decline in their numbers from over exploitation, competition from non-native species that have entered the waters, making it one of the more threatened marine creatures in Europe. There are two hundred species of this mollusk and throughout history it has been used for making and creating structures such as castles, building roads and as a beauty product as well as a food source.

In and around the estuaries of river Blackwater and the Crouch the native oyster ostrea edulis more commonly known as the flat oyster dwells. Currently in Essex a restoration initiative is taking place to create a sustainable and ecosystem for these oysters and to support the riverbed in helping it to assist the life forms of sea urchins, small fish, and spats to provide a nursery for them to grow. Returning the shells to the ocean is important for restoring the oyster reefs. Oysters' shells with their rich mineral composition can also be used as compost, mulch though expert agreed it is best to boil them as this sterilise them and removes the buildup of sea salt naturally found on them. Clean shells make an excellent additive and help improve the effectiveness of the soil with their ability to raise the pH level in the soil when they take up the micronutrients of zinc, iron, and manganese from the oyster shell remnants. The leftover shells can also be given to livestock and in the past were used to make cement to construct buildings. This was known as 'Tabby,' where concrete was made by burning oyster shells to create lime then mixed with water, sand and ash and broken oyster shells. Lucy had seen the remains of this at Colchester castle. The shells were also and still are made into decorative pieces of jewellery. The oldest said to be over hundred thousand years old from Skhul in Israel.

In Greek mythology Aphrodite, born from the foam of the sea caused by Cronus castrating his father Uranus genitals and throwing them into the ocean and out of the raging sea Aphrodite emerged as she travelled to land on an oyster or clam shell, it is said she shed a tear and a pearl was formed. Oysters are associated with pearls; The first recorded pearl in history was by a Chinese historian in 2300 BC.

Though pearls are classed as gemstones, unlike other precious stones they are not found beneath the earth's surface but are organically produced in nature being formed from various freshwater or saltwater mollusks. However, only one in ten thousand oysters will produce a pearl taking on average three years to make, as not all oysters will develop a pearl. The tiny pearl inside the shell comes from a non-living organism or parasite known as an irritant. which in beds itself into the mantle of a living oyster. The oyster layers the irritant in nacre as a form of self-defense to protect itself. From this a pearl is formed. Lucy was unsure if she could call the irritants in her life precious gems, oh they had taught her a lot and they had been annoying and at times cruel. Lucy was silent for a moment and considered the possibility of her licking the emotional pain with her tears to create a protective friendship of admiration in the relationship between this symbolic relationship of love and hate. It is said all relationships we encounter are to teach us, guide us or protect us.

Pearls are strongly connected to the feminine throughout history and are symbols of fertility, purity, determination, perfection, and romance. We also must be reminded of the opposing side of the feminine characteristic of revengefulness, gossip, and hostility when we feel threatened, betrayed, or harmed. Evidence has shown in history the brutality women have had against each other.

In western culture they are associated with the planet Venus in astrology as the saltwater pearls produce a soft white orb that is said to create the shape of the moon, hence the connection to the moon. The freshwater pearls do not produce the soft silk roundness of the saltwater and create their own unique shapes and markings. During ancient times kings and the ruling class wore strings of pearls as a sign of wealth and was forbidden to be worn by the lower classes.

Even throughout history pearls have played a part in the lives of the rich and famous as they were attributed to confidence, prestige, and personal strength. More importantly they are associated with love and romance, often given traditionally to celebrate a thirtieth wedding anniversary. They were given to females, or wives as a sign of purity, honesty, and wisdom and long lasting and solid bonds in the courtship of their relationship. Interestingly Lucy noted pearls were one of the oldest traditions among brides and were worn during the Ancient Greek and Roman times as a sign of a happy marriage. They are also associated with those people born in the month of June representing innocence and sincerity. In Chinese culture it was believed the birthstone came from the brain of a dragon.

Lucy wondered where the notion that the oyster was considered an aphrodisiac was. It certainly did nothing for her and most people she had spoken to about this subject were of the same opinion. Lucy was more than aware that the zinc was useful for the male's libido and considered this the possibility of why the Romans enjoyed them so much, that the euphoric feeling obtained from eating these oysters provided them with prowess and determination on the battlefield. Testosterone not only creates sex drive, but it also develops bone mass, muscle size and strength. It also helps with red blood cell production and fat distribution. When the Romans found the same type of oyster in the estuary as back home in the Mediterranean, they were incredibly happy as unlike the Mediterranean Sea these oysters were on a tidal system and were easier to harvest than back home, allowing them to indulge.

Today as Lucy looked out across the sea, she realised her brother all those years ago had scattered their mothers' ashes at one of Hekate's crossroads. The meeting point of the earth, sea, and sky. Lucy always felt her mother was lost and needed direction and now here was Hekate guiding her through the underworld to her resting place. Since leaving England, Lucy had done much soul searching. It had not been easy and in truth she was still working through her pain and trauma. Recognition of your failings and acknowledging your past can be quite traumatic. Lucy had known for quite a while it had been time to release the past.

Chapter Fourteen

Nehalennia

'She of the sea., guide me, protect me on my voyage as I circumnavigate life's journey.'

The river Crouch eventually makes its way out to the North Sea. At some point in history, it is suggested the Romans brought the Goddess Nehalennia with them as they crossed the treacherous sea between Europe and the British Isles. Lucy had travelled across this sea many times on day trips and never perceived it as treacherous or even dangerous. Though she did have to admit in the winter months it had been unpleasant, and she had been quite sick over the choppy waters of the channel between home and France. Although for Lucy it did not take much to make her queasy. She had even managed to throw up on the toddler rides when she had accompanied her young son on a ride at a local fairground. Since that day Lucy had avoided all rides at fairs and theme parks. She certainly did not have the constitution to stomach them.

Nehalennia was Dutch in origin and her name meant 'she of the sea.' Nehalennia was considered popular among seafarers and her statue or markings were carved on the bow of ships and in honour of her loaves of sweetbread named duivekater were made into the shape of a bone to represent animals and were given as a sacrifice offering. For all of those who sailed the seas and worked as ship workers and merchants. She, Nehalennia was their protector and guide during the transit. It is believed Nehalennia at one time in history had a strong influence in the Flanders region of North Europe. In the town of Zeeland three hundred and seventy votive were discovered with inscriptions, prayers and devotions dating back to the early third centuries CE. No one is certain of her heritage or her origins, but two altars were found in the region of Cologne, Germany dating back to the second and third century. It is thought she was Germanic Celtic though; this cannot be agreed upon. What we do know is when the tribes from the Flanders region of Northern Europe emigrated to the British Isles, they brought Nehalennia with them.

At Nehalennia's right side sat a hound, thought to be a greyhound. Greyhounds are thought to be the oldest purebred dog in the world and date back to the time of Pharaoh. They were revered by gods, royalty, and literature scholars such as Homer and Shakespeare. It is thanks to priests and monks during the dark ages the breed was saved from extinction.

What we do know about Nehalennia there was a connection to the underworld and like Hekate guided those who were deceased across to the other side. On her lap was a basket or corpus of apples, some think she may have had pomegranate which are connected to the underworld, others believed the basket to be filled with apples. Like pomegranate, apples are associated with the underworld. When cutting crossways, a pentagram or a five-pointed star is formed in the centre of the apple. The pentagram represents the five elements of our natural world Aether/Void/Spirit that encompasses all space and time of our existence, Air, Water, Fire, and Earth. For eons it has been used to represent spiritual as well as religious beliefs and ideology. In astrology our signs are broken down into elements and depending on our sign we are seen as being brash, logical, quick tempered, emotional, practical, airheaded, and even grounded. Each one of us is a little bit more complex than being one genre, I for one am known to be practical, very much of a home body. I am also extremely critical and evaluate every detail to excess, that I miss opportunities as I seek perfection (Earth). Also, part of my nature is to keep order, especially in relationships and there is a need for balance, like Maat the Egyptian goddess of truth balance, order, and harmony. Who measured everyone's heart with that of her feather (Air). Knowing it is impossible to be perfect and to find true equilibrium of everlasting balance in this world, I can also find myself being overwhelmed and torture myself in my lack of pursuit to idealise and fix what cannot be. Though the state of probability drives me to imagine I can (Water).

The apple tree is said to grow in the underworld providing food for the dead during the chilly winter months. Apples are the food of love and death with its unique relationship between its association of evil in the story of snow white, the forbidden fruit in the garden of Eden resulting in Eve's banishment from the garden, The apple is and always will be in history a sign of immortality. It is believed the gods of Greek; Roman and Christian beliefs humans were given the apple as a warning not to be taken in by things that we see as advantageous and to have it removed from us. The apple tree is customary known for its eternal love, abundance, and good health for the future. Especially in females where it represented the womb and ovaries.

Like Persephone and Kore, the apple or pomegranate is also representative of our character of letting go of the maiden, our youthful innocence and stepping into our queendom. To seek change and to be the change. As we grow it brings with it chaos, confrontations, and lessons all which Kore and Persephone faced.

The apple tree was also known for being the tree of love and its fruit the apple was used in divination for communication and connection. Just like Hekate and other witches and goddesses, Nehalennia transcended between worlds reaching into the underworld, the earthly realm and that of the upper world. Nehalennia had strong ties to water and as a mother goddess had the ability to give new life in the new world or was Nehalennia with her loaves of bread and dog by her side and having the ability to transcend to liminal spaces another version of Hekate manifestation upon the world. This we will never know. Much like Morrigan and Hekate, Nehalennia was the goddess of the dead and as such she was patron of the home and hearth. One thing we can be certain in life, is death is much a part of life as is birth. It is guaranteed.

Though the air was cold the sky was a bright cobalt blue and yacht racing was taking place on the crouch. Day visitors like herself watched on from the shoreline, she admired the tenacity each sailor had in handling the masts and navigating the waters. As Lucy looked out across the river crouch to the North Sea, she felt the sense of freedom and release come over her, she was no longer anyone's daughter, nor was she tied to the past.

Guidance

O Hekate
As I enter the darkness
stand beside me.
Not as friend
Nor as foe
But as my guide
To the things I must face
About myself
To see my path
To see the truth of who I am.
To stand at the crossroad
And observe.
The past, present and future
The path is mine alone to take.
In this darkness, there is light.
I must choose.
Which way to go
To meet my true self.

By Carla Peters

Originally from UK, Carla emigrated to Australia and now lives in Queensland with her family. When Carla is not working as a nurse, she loves to spend her time with her family and her beloved animals, connecting into nature, immersing herself in the spiritual world, and writing poetry.

.

www.ingramcontent.com/pod-product-compliance
Lightning Source LLC
Chambersburg PA
CBHW070309010526
44107CB00056B/2541